Working
for Myself

THE FLOWER MAN

Tana Reiff

LAKE EDUCATION

Belmont, California

Working for Myself

Cooking for a Crowd
You Call, We Haul
Your Kids and Mine
Other People's Pets
The Green Team
Clean as a Whistle
Beauty and the Business
Handy All Around
Crafting a Business

Cover Illustration: James Balkovek
Cover Design: Ina McInnis
Text Designer: Diann Abbott

Library of Congress Catalog Number: 94-076148
ISBN 1-56103-910-1
Printed in the United States of America
1 9 8 7 6 5 4 3 2 1

CONTENTS

Chapter

C H A P T E R 1

The Power Chair

Today it was a packing job. Victor Marks sat at his work station and packed candles one by one into a box. When that box was full, he moved it down the line and packed another. And then another. And another.

He watched the woman across the table from him. She worked so fast. She'd make a lot more money today than Victor would.

"Well, that's piece work," he said to himself. "You get paid by how much you do. It's a good deal for that woman, but not for me. I'm working as hard as I can, but I just can't work as fast as she does."

This week it was packing candles in a box. Next week it might be shrink-wrapping cards for the gift shop. The workshop took whatever jobs came in. Victor didn't find any of the work interesting. Every day he was afraid his mind might go to sleep—and the rest of him, too.

The pay was very low. "But I'm lucky to have a job," Victor told himself again and again. Lots of people in town were out of work. His own father had been laid off a month ago. And a person in a wheelchair can't pick and choose jobs all that easily. Victor felt lucky to be getting a regular paycheck.

Victor had wanted to do something other than this after high school. He hadn't decided exactly what. But then his parents moved to this town to be near his father's mother. Victor didn't know anyone here who could help him find a good job.

So he had called the state rehab office. They put him in touch with the workshop. The place employed people who were disabled in some way. The workshop people talked to him. Victor wasn't sure they asked the right questions. He wasn't sure he gave the best answers. But they were nice people, and they had a job for him.

Victor never missed a day of work. Even though he was bored, he sat at his station week after week. But he always felt there was more inside him.

He never wheeled much beyond the nearest men's room or the exit door. His arms were strong, but his chair had no motor. And there was nothing much to do or see anywhere else in the workshop. The only place he wanted to go was outside. He longed to breathe fresh air and see the clear blue sky.

Then the rehab office did something that would change Victor's life. They called to say they could get Victor a new wheelchair—*a power chair*! It had a motor built right into it. Victor would be able to buzz all over the place at the touch of a button. And a power chair was almost as light as a feather.

Victor had tried a friend's power wheelchair once. It was too small for him, but Victor liked the feel of it. Ever since then he had wanted his own power chair. To Victor, this news was a dream come true.

The first day with his new chair, Victor came to work just as he always did. He sat at his station just as he always did. He packed candles in boxes. Nothing was different.

Then it came time for him to go to the men's bathroom. Victor could have gone to the nearest one, the way he always had. But instead, he headed for the larger men's room in another department down at the end of the hall.

What he saw there shocked him. The people in that room were taking candles *out* of boxes!

Victor put it all together. The people in his department packed the candles. The people in the other department unpacked them. Then the people in his department packed the same candles all over again.

That did it. Victor went from the men's room to the counselor's office. "What's going on here?" he asked. "I can't believe it. One room is packing candles, and the very next room is unpacking them. Are we all doing the same thing over and over for nothing?"

The counselor, Ms. Singleton, tried to explain. "Believe me, Victor, this doesn't happen often," she said. "But we do have slow times. Then we have to *make* work so you can keep on getting paid. Do you understand?"

"I understand that it's time for me to move on," Victor said. "Look, I'm grateful for the job you've given me," he added. "But I'm bored. And I know I'm capable of doing work that is more . . . well, interesting."

"That's fine, Victor," said Ms. Singleton. "We're happy when people here move into jobs outside the workshop. Let's talk about what you would like to do."

"I'd like to work for myself," said Victor. "Maybe I want too much, but that's what I want to do."

So Ms. Singleton asked Victor a lot of questions. They were both surprised by some of his answers.

Wheelchair or not, Victor Marks very much wanted to be out on his own. Wheelchair or not, he wanted to work outdoors. Wheelchair or not, he wanted to deal with people. And wheelchair or not, he wanted every day to be different.

It all added up. Ms. Singleton didn't

have to tell Victor. He already knew what he wanted. "I want to be a street vendor," he said. "I don't know what I want to sell. But I want to get out into the world. I want to see the sky and feel the sun on my face. I want to hear the car horns. I want to talk to people every day. I want to run my own business."

CHAPTER 2

A Busy Mind

"A street vendor? Have you lost your mind?" Victor's mother said to him that night at home.

"Do you know how many businesses go under in the first year?" his father asked. "And you want to quit the workshop to start your own business? You're *dreaming*!"

"Businesses fail for lots of reasons," Victor said. "A disability isn't usually one of them. Look. I know I can do much more than I'm doing now. Maybe I won't get rich. But I can enjoy my work more. Doesn't that count for something?"

"You call selling on the street *fun*?" said Mr. Marks.

"It *could* be fun," said Victor.

"What makes you think you'd be better off?" said Mrs. Marks. "Think about those blind men who sell newspapers. People buy papers because they feel sorry for those men."

"Maybe they *do* feel sorry for them," said Victor. "But people also buy papers because they want papers."

"So what do you want to sell?" said Mrs. Marks.

"I don't know yet, Mother. Maybe flowers."

"Flowers!" Mr. Marks said with a huff. "What kind of money could you make selling flowers?"

"Well, I don't think I can sell food," said Victor. "I don't think I could handle a pushcart. But I think I could sit in my chair and sell flowers. And there's plenty of money to be made selling flowers."

"It would be harder than you think," said Mrs. Marks.

"I read about a guy with one arm who built his own house," said Victor. "That man could hammer nails and everything. Think about it, Mother. If a guy with one arm can build a house, I sure as heck can sell flowers."

"You might have a lot of problems running your own business," Mrs. Marks said. "How are you going to deal with a problem from a wheelchair?"

"You know what they say about problems," Victor said. "If you can't go through them, go around them. And I can do *everything* better with my new power chair." He buzzed across the living room in seconds.

"Hey, you're lightning on wheels, aren't you?" laughed Mr. Marks.

"Give the boy a break," said Mrs.

Marks. "Maybe he's right. Maybe he knows what he can do a lot better than we do."

Victor could feel his parents giving in. At least his mother. No one spoke for a few minutes. Then Victor said, "How's this? I won't quit my job at the workshop until I get my new business off the ground. If I can't make it on my own, I'll still have my old job."

Victor's mother turned to look at his father. Then she looked back at Victor. "That's fair," she said.

"What about you, Dad? What do you say?" Victor asked.

"It's two against one," said Mr. Marks. "Go ahead. But you'll have to do it yourself. I've got to hit the streets every day looking for my own job. Don't ask me for any help."

Victor didn't sleep a wink that night. His mind was full of ideas. He thought about how and where he would set up his stand. He thought about how he would get the flowers and the best way to show them. And he thought about how he'd get where he needed to go in his wonderful power chair.

The next morning Victor called the workshop. He told his boss that he wouldn't be in that day.

Victor's father wasn't around to drive him where he wanted to go. And his mother was working the day shift. So Victor buzzed his chair to the nearest bus stop. He wanted to take a little trip around the area. He wanted to look for busy corners. Somewhere there had to be the perfect corner for his flower stand.

Victor wasn't used to taking the bus. A special van picked him up every morning to take him to the workshop. It had a wheelchair lift that made it easy for him to get on and off.

Victor waited 15 minutes. At last a bus pulled over. Victor waited for the driver to let down the wheelchair lift in the back. But it didn't happen.

"Sorry, buddy!" the driver called down to him. "This bus doesn't have a lift. The 7:15 has one, but you missed it. The next bus with a lift comes at 10:00."

So Victor waited. The 10:00 bus was late, but the lift worked fine. Victor sat by a window and looked closely at every street. He kept a sharp eye out for busy street corners.

While the bus stopped at a red light, Victor spotted something he wasn't even looking for. At first he thought it was a big flower shop. Then he saw the sign: "Wholesale Flowers." It was a company that sells flowers to flower shops. He copied down the address. He wanted to talk to these people.

At the next light, Victor saw what he was looking for. It was a busy crossroads. Cars and more cars stopped at the lights on all four sides. On one corner there was an empty lot. A small building sat back from the road. This was perfect! And it was only three blocks from the wholesale flower place. What could be better?

"Hey, driver! Do you know anything about that empty lot on the corner?" Victor asked. "What used to be there?"

"It used to be a used car lot," said the driver. "I don't know who owns it."

"Let me off at the county office, please," Victor told him. "I'm going to find out."

CHAPTER 3

Making Deals

The county deed records said the lot belonged to a man by the name of Ralph Houseman. Victor wrote down Mr. Houseman's phone number. Then he asked permission to use the phone. He was lucky enough to reach Mr. Houseman right away.

"My name is Victor Marks," he said. "I see in the county deed records that you own a lot at the corner of Route 20 and

Wood Street."

"Yes, I do," said Mr. Houseman. "I had a used car business renting that lot from me for a while. They went out of business. Are you interested in renting the lot yourself?"

"I'd like to sell flowers on your lot," said Victor. "I only need the corner. I was wondering if we could work out some kind of a deal."

"Well, I don't know," said Mr. Houseman. "How much would you be able to pay me?"

"I don't have any money right now," Victor explained. "I was thinking that maybe I could pay you 10 percent of whatever I clear on the flowers."

"That could be a lot or a little," Mr. Houseman laughed.

"That's right," said Victor, not laughing. "I *hope* it's a lot. I plan to make a go of this business."

"Well, I have to pay taxes on that lot whether anybody's using it or not. Right now I'm not making peanuts on it," said Mr. Houseman. "So I guess 10 percent of something is better than nothing—for now. But if someone comes along to rent the whole lot, I couldn't turn down an offer. Do you understand that? Give me your address and I'll send you a lease."

"A lease? I need a lease?"

"Yes. There are certain conditions for renting. For example, I want to make sure you won't leave trash or anything on my property," said Mr. Houseman. "Understand?"

That sounded fair to Victor.

Then Mr. Houseman added, "But first you need to get approval from the zoning office. I can't sign a lease until you get your zoning permit."

Victor said he would call back after he contacted the zoning office. Then he hung up the phone. He hadn't said a word to Mr. Houseman about his being in a wheelchair.

Zoning permits were not issued at the

county office. For the zoning department, Victor would have to go to the township office. But just now he was feeling tired. It had been a busy day already. So he waited for a bus with a lift and headed home.

Victor couldn't take off work again the next day. But the following Monday morning he rode the bus to the township office.

Victor wasn't sure what zoning laws were. He thought they had something to do with how the land and buildings in different neighborhoods could be used. He was right. The woman at the zoning office explained the laws. One type of zone was an area set aside for apartments and houses. Another was set aside for factories. Another could be used to set up stores and other businesses.

"You're asking to sell flowers in a business zone," the woman said. "That's right in line with the zoning law. Just fill out this form."

It took Victor some time to do that. He filled in the information as neatly as he could. Then he handed the form back to the woman.

"That's fine," she said. "Now all you need is a business license."

First a lease, then a zoning paper, and now a business license! Victor was beginning to think there was no end to the paperwork. "But I've already come a long way," he said to himself. "I can't stop now."

So he buzzed his chair down the hall to the next office. The woman there gave him another form to fill out. It was almost noon when Victor finished that one.

"Very good," said the woman. "Now all I need is 50 dollars and you're in business."

Victor just about fell out of his chair. "I didn't know I would have to pay *that* much for a business license!" he said. "I only have a few dollars on me right now."

"Well, I'm sorry, sir," said the woman. "But I can't stamp this license until I have a check for 50 dollars."

Victor looked away. "Where on earth am I going to get 50 dollars?" he said under his breath. To Victor, the woman might as well have asked for 1,000 dollars.

Victor could think of only one place where he could possibly get the money. That was from his father. But he had not forgotten his father's words: "Don't ask me for any help."

He thought about selling flowers *without* a business license. He was sure that some other street vendors worked that way. But no. He knew that Mr. Houseman would want everything on the up and up. And deep down, so did Victor.

Victor looked up at the woman. "Thank you," he said. "I guess I'll have to come back another time."

CHAPTER 4

A Will and a Way

Everyone at the workshop was shrink-wrapping cards that week. It was Tuesday—three days until the weekend. To Victor, it seemed like a hundred days. Every hour dragged by slowly.

All he could think about was the 50 dollars that he needed. The difference between working in the workshop and having his own flower stand was 50 dollars. Victor was a cheerful person. He had never felt very sorry for himself because he lived in a wheelchair. But this week was different. When he saw people driving nice cars and wearing nice clothes, he felt bad. To them, 50 dollars was not very much at all. To Victor, it was everything.

On Saturday morning he couldn't stand thinking about it anymore. "Dad," he said, "can you lend me 50 dollars for a business license? I promise to pay you back with the first 50 dollars I make."

"If you can't come up with 50 dollars, how are you going to buy flowers to get started?" said Mr. Marks. "How will you get this business going without money?"

"I was hoping that you could help me," Victor said softly.

"I'm sorry, Victor. The answer is no," Mr. Marks said. "I told you I couldn't help. If you need money, why don't you go to the bank?"

A bank loan. "Who would give me a loan?" Victor thought to himself. "Still, what could it hurt to ask? I guess it would be worth a try."

On Monday morning Victor went to the bank. There he was matched up with a loan officer. It was this man's job to work with small businesses. The loan officer helped Victor make up a list of everything he would need to get started. It added up to more money than Victor had expected. Still, it would not be a big loan.

The loan officer asked Victor a lot of questions. Would the people at the workshop say that he was honest? Did he come to work on time? Did he stick with things or give up easily? Was he strong enough? Would he have the energy to get a hard job done? Victor thought these were good questions. It was important for the bank to know these things about anyone going into business.

The next few questions, though, were just for someone with a disability. Could he take care of himself on an empty lot? Could he get to his corner without being able to drive? What would he do if people said they felt sorry for him? These questions were harder to answer.

Then came the hardest question of all. The bank wanted some kind of guarantee. What could Victor put up for the bank to take if he didn't pay back his loan?

"I don't know," Victor answered.

"Think," said the loan officer. "What do you own that's worth money?"

Victor owned only one thing that was worth any real money.

"I *will* pay back the loan," he said. "But if for some reason I don't—you can take my wheelchair."

For the first time, Victor saw pity on the loan officer's face. Then the man looked down and wrote the words *power wheelchair* on the loan form. "We'll check your references," he said. "I'll let you know in a day or two."

Two days later Victor got the loan. He paid the township 50 dollars and got his business license. He signed a lease with Mr. Houseman. Then he made one more deal. This one was with the wholesale flower business up the street from the empty lot. Finally, he bought some lumber to build his flower stand.

He got the lumber yard to deliver the wood to the house. He began working with a saw and hammer. His parents watched him from the window. They saw what a hard time he was having. Victor's mother was almost in tears.

Finally, after watching for a long time, Victor's father came outside.

"Nothing is going to stop you, is it, son?" Mr. Marks said.

Victor looked up at his father. From where Victor sat, his father seemed tall, even though he really wasn't. "I have to make my way in the world," he said. "I'm willing to do whatever it takes."

"Do you want some help?" Mr. Marks

asked. He picked up the saw. He laid a board across two tree stumps. Then he drew a line and sawed straight along it. Together, he and Victor sanded the edges. He held the nails while Victor hammered. In no time at all, the stack of boards became a long, sturdy table.

"Thanks, Dad," Victor said. "I sure wish I could—but I just *can't* do everything myself."

"I couldn't watch you fighting that board," said Mr. Marks. "So what are you going to sell from this table?"

"I worked out a good deal with a wholesaler," Victor said. "It's a company that sells flowers to flower shops. They're going to sell me cut flowers at a very low price. I'll buy the extra flowers that they would have to throw out."

"That does sound like a good deal," said Mr. Marks. "How are you going to set up the flowers on your table here?"

"I'm going to keep them in jars of water. When someone buys a bunch, I'll wrap them in green paper."

"Where are you going to put the money?" Mr. Marks asked.

"That I don't know yet," Victor said.

"I have an old tackle box," said Mr. Marks. "It's still in good shape. I never go fishing anymore. Do you want to use it for a money box?"

"That would be perfect," said Victor.

Then the two of them painted a big sign. "FLOWERS FOR SALE," it said, in big red letters.

C H A P T E R 5

Mother's Day

It was the nicest, brightest day of spring. It was Mother's Day. Victor Marks sat on the corner of Route 20 and Wood Street. In front of him was a table full of flowers. Buds of red roses and bunches of flowers of all colors caught the morning sun. They looked beautiful.

It was Victor's first day in business. He chose Mother's Day because he knew that many people bought flowers as gifts.

He was sure this would be a fine start for his business. The stand was all ready. The set-up work was behind him. Now flowers by the dozens covered the long tabletop. Victor was feeling very proud of himself.

His big sign was next to his table. No one who drove by could miss that sign. And it seemed as if no one did miss it.

Car after car pulled over. One after another, people bought bunches of Victor's flowers. "Who's the lucky lady getting flowers today?" Victor would say. People would answer, "My wife," or "My mother," or "My daughter."

All morning long people stopped by and bought flowers. By noon Victor's table was empty.

That was good news—and bad. Victor thought he had bought plenty of flowers for the whole day. Now he saw that he didn't have enough. He could have sold many more. Then Victor had an idea.

He buzzed his chair across the side

street and found a pay phone. He wanted to call Wholesale Flowers. He knew it was Sunday. But the lady there said they always stayed open on Mother's Day.

Victor buzzed his chair right up next to the phone. He pulled a quarter out of his jacket pocket. But he couldn't reach up far enough. The phone was six inches from his fingertips.

The morning had been so much fun. He had a tackle box full of money! But now he felt terrible—all because he couldn't reach a phone.

He tried to lift himself out of the chair far enough to grab the phone. He couldn't do it. He sank back into the chair. The quarter fell out of his hand and rolled away.

Then he thought of the tackle box. "How stupid can you get?" he told himself. He had left the box full of money back at the stand! Anyone could have walked right up and taken it.

Victor buzzed the chair back across the

street as fast as he could. The tackle box was still under the table where he had left it! He took out some change and put it in his pocket.

Then he had an idea. The tackle box was about six inches high. Six inches was all he needed to reach the phone. If he could somehow get the tackle box under his seat . . .

Victor pulled himself up by his arms. With one arm he held himself up off the chair. With the other arm he quickly pushed the tackle box onto the chair seat. Then he sat on top of it.

Now he was sitting very high in his chair. Maybe too high. He knew it was a bit dangerous to run the chair when he was sitting like that. But he had to give it a try.

Holding on tightly, he buzzed the chair back across the street. He pulled the chair up to the phone again. He reached into his pocket for money. Then he reached right up, dropped the coin into the slot, and dialed the number of Wholesale Flowers.

Victor was lucky. The woman at the order desk answered right away. "We still have cut flowers," she said. "But they're not day-old ones. They're the very fresh flowers we were going to use tomorrow. I will have to charge you full price."

Victor was shocked when he heard how high the price was. It was *much* more than he had paid yesterday for the day-old flowers.

He had to think fast. Could he sell the flowers for more than he would pay for them? Yes, he thought he could.

"I'll take them," he said. "And I need some more green paper, OK?"

"You got it," said the woman. "The van is on its way."

While he waited, Victor ate the lunch he had packed. In 20 minutes, his table was full of flowers once again. He was back in business.

Victor sold flowers for three more

hours. He didn't make very much on this second batch. Still, it was more than he would have made if he had packed up and gone home.

Victor was very tired at the end of that busy day. But he didn't care. His tackle box was full of cash! It was worth two sore arms and a sore neck. He did wonder how he would feel tomorrow. He would have to be up bright and early to go to the workshop. After working his shift, he would take the bus back to the stand. He had to be ready to sell flowers again at the 5:00 rush hour.

He knew he had to stick with it, though. As each customer had left his stand that day, Victor had made a promise. He had smiled and said, "Starting tomorrow you can look for me every day after work. I'll be here."

When Victor got home, he gave his father 40 dollars. He knew he didn't have to. But he also knew how worried his father was about finding work. Maybe

Mr. Marks could use the extra money to buy groceries or pay a bill. Victor felt proud to be *giving* help instead of taking help. But mostly he wanted to show his father that his business was for real.

CHAPTER 6

Solving Problems

Victor was glad that he had started on Mother's Day. That day had showed him how *good* things could be. But not every day was a big flower holiday.

The next few days showed him how *most* days would be. Victor left the workshop at 3:30 P.M. He took a bus to the corner of Route 20 and Wood Street. The Wholesale Flowers van got to his stand at 4:00.

Then Victor put together mixed bunches from many different kinds of flowers. For each bunch he gathered up two yellows, two whites, two pinks, and one purple. Then he put a band around them. He separated the roses into half dozens and dozens. He lined up all the flowers in jars. Around 5:00 the customers started pulling over.

When night fell, Victor threw out the leftover flowers and put the jars under the table. About the same time, his father came to pick him up.

Not every day went well. Sometimes there weren't many customers at all. But the biggest problem was the bus from the workshop. The first bus that came by that stop didn't always have a wheelchair lift. Ms. Singleton called the bus company about it.

But even after she called, Victor often had to wait an extra half-hour or more for a bus with a lift. Whenever that happened, he couldn't be ready in time for the 5:00 customers. He hated waiting at the bus stop. It cost him an hour when he could be at his stand selling flowers.

The weather was another problem. Most days were clear and warm. But it was spring. In this part of the country, spring was a rainy season.

The first time it rained, people still stopped to buy flowers. But Victor got wet. He just couldn't hold an umbrella and wrap flowers at the same time. The water dripped down his face, and his clothes got soaked.

The next time it rained, Victor wore a cap. It didn't help much. But it did give him an idea. Victor still had some money left from his bank loan. He decided to use part of it to buy a big beach umbrella. His father helped him build a special stand for it. The umbrella helped a lot.

If it was raining, or if the sun beat down too hard, Victor could pull on a cord to open the umbrella. In the rain, the umbrella kept him dry. In the sun, the umbrella kept him a little cooler.

That umbrella was the second best thing to happen since he'd gotten the power chair! Victor no longer had to worry about the weather.

By the middle of summer, Victor felt that he had things under control. He enjoyed the work. He had a happy word for every customer. People started calling him "the flower man."

Still, his days were very long. It was very tiring to work all day at the workshop and then sell flowers until dark. Victor didn't know how much longer he could do both jobs. Some days he fell asleep on the bus ride to his flower stand. Still, he kept going—day in and day out. And he spent longer hours at the stand on weekends.

In the fall, Victor took his biggest step yet. He quit his job at the workshop.

"We're going to miss you, Victor," Ms. Singleton told him. "You've been a very good worker, even if you didn't like it here. We wish you the best of luck!"

On his last day, Victor brought in a flower for each person at the workshop. He gave Ms. Singleton a dozen roses. She gave Victor a hug.

Then he was gone. From now on there would be no more packing boxes. No more shrink-wrapping. And no more steady paycheck.

Quitting the workshop gave Victor a lot more time at the flower stand. He sold more flowers and made more money. And now he wasn't so tired all the time.

Only now, getting home at night became a problem. His father had taken a night job. He couldn't pick Victor up anymore. And Victor just couldn't count on catching a bus with a lift. Sometimes he had to take a taxi home. But a taxi ride cost too much money. Besides, it was hard to use the phone to call a cab.

Then Victor came up with another bright idea.

He called the state rehab office. He

explained his problem to a woman there. "I was wondering if a van with a wheelchair lift could pick me up after work," he said.

"Why, sure!" said the woman on the phone. "We take lots of people to and from work. What time? Where? Do you need a ride to get to work, too?"

Before he knew it, Victor had set up a van ride both to and from work. He couldn't believe it. The problem was so hard, but the answer was so easy. Whenever he really needed help, it seemed that he got it. Sometimes all he had to do was ask.

CHAPTER 7

Storing More Flowers

Victor didn't mind throwing away the leftover flowers at the end of the day. He paid very little for them. He knew that he wasn't really losing money.

Then the weather grew colder. The cool air was keeping the flowers in good enough condition to sell the next day. Victor hated to throw away good flowers. He wished he had a way to keep them cool any time of the year.

Victor had noticed a small building at the back of the lot. Mr. Houseman said it had been the office for the used car salespeople. One day Victor wheeled over to take a look at it.

The door was locked. The window was boarded up. But there was a crack between the boards. It was just large enough for Victor to peek through and see what was inside.

Even though it was dark, Victor thought he saw an outlet in the wall. He could picture a refrigerator plugged in there. He could picture it full of his left-over flowers.

That night, Victor made a phone call to Mr. Houseman.

"Is there electric power inside that little building on your lot?" Victor asked his landlord.

"Yes, but it's been turned off," said Mr. Houseman.

"Well, I'd like to make you another deal," said Victor. "If you have the power turned back on, I could set up a big refrigerator in there. I'd pay the electric bill and give you 15 percent of whatever I clear on the flowers."

"That's fine," said Mr. Houseman. "You've been a good tenant so far. And I'm happy to make the extra money. But—and I don't mean to second-guess you, Victor—will you be able to pay me that much more?"

"I think so. Let's see how it goes," Victor said. "Thanks."

"I'll be over this afternoon," said Mr. Houseman.

In all these months, Victor and Mr. Houseman had never met face to face. Mr. Houseman had never come by to check on his lot. He was shocked when he saw Victor.

"I had no idea that you were in a wheelchair!" Mr. Houseman said. "Well, aren't you brave! Just imagine running a business from a wheelchair!"

"I'm not brave," said Victor. "I'm just

living with a disability."

"Right," said Mr. Houseman. "I didn't mean that as a put-down."

"That's OK," said Victor.

"Well, now I think even more of you," Mr. Houseman said.

With that, he gave Victor a key to the office. He said that he had talked to the power company. They would turn on the electricity in the morning.

Victor bought a used refrigerator. He started keeping extra flowers in it right away. Every day he made sure that he sold the oldest flowers first.

Having the refrigerator was even more useful than Victor had thought. On some days, Wholesale Flowers had extra flowers to sell him. Now Victor could buy more flowers at a low cost when he had the money. By keeping them for a day or two, he almost never ran out. He still had to throw old flowers away sometimes. But he almost never had to buy new flowers at full price anymore.

Then Victor came up with a way to get some use out of his leftover flowers. A woman named Mrs. Dixon stopped in every Thursday. She always bought flowers to put on her mother's grave.

"What do you do with your extra flowers?" she asked one day.

"I keep them in a refrigerator as long as possible," Victor explained. "But once in a while I still have to throw some out."

"Well, I have an idea," Mrs. Dixon said. "Every time I visit my mother's grave, I see many other graves with no flowers on them. Could I buy up your extras at a low price? It might be nice to leave flowers on those bare graves."

"No, no," said Victor. "I wouldn't want to take money for throwaway flowers. You can just take whatever I have left over. I'd be happy to let you have them."

So Victor started saving the old flowers. Every Thursday when Mrs. Dixon stopped by, she bought flowers for her mother's grave. Then she loaded her car trunk with the flowers that Victor would have thrown out. Every Thursday afternoon she laid the free flowers on the graves of people she didn't know.

That month, Victor sold a lot more flowers. He was sure it was because of the refrigerator. He figured out what he had to pay Mr. Houseman. He paid the electric bill. Then he saw how much was left to keep. It was *less* than before he'd gotten the refrigerator!

At first Victor thought he had given Mrs. Dixon too many free flowers. Then he studied the figures and saw what had happened. Giving more to Mr. Houseman and paying the electric bill was costing more than he thought.

Victor didn't want to give up the office. He decided to wait a few more months. He hoped that somehow things would turn around.

Then one Thursday, Victor showed up early at the stand. As the van pulled away, he looked out on the busy intersection. A very big surprise was waiting there for him. It was a woman, standing at the corner of Route 20 and Wood Street. She was selling flowers!

CHAPTER 8

A Growing Business

"Excuse me," Victor said politely to the woman, "but I have a city license to sell flowers on this corner. I'm afraid you'll have to leave."

The woman looked down at Victor in his wheelchair. Her face was cold and hard. "Make me," was all she said.

Victor couldn't believe the woman had said that. "Do I have to go to the township about this?" Victor asked her.

"I guess you do," she answered.

So, while the woman sold flowers on Victor's corner, Victor waited at the bus stop across the street.

He waited and waited. Every now and then he looked over at the woman. He saw cars pulling over to buy flowers from her. He was so angry, he thought he would burst.

Then he spotted Mrs. Dixon's car. It was Thursday, and she had come to get her flowers.

"Mrs. Dixon!" Victor called from the other side of the street. He waved his arms in the air to get her attention.

Victor saw his favorite customer talking to the woman on his corner. He was sure that Mrs. Dixon was asking where he was. The flower woman was shaking her head as if to say *no*.

"Mrs. Dixon!" Victor called again. This time she heard him.

"There you are!" she called over.

Then she got back into her car and

drove over to Victor's side of the street.

"What's going on?" she asked him.

Victor explained.

"Let's get you into my car," she said. "We'll get this straightened out!"

Mrs. Dixon was far from a young woman. It was hard for her to help Victor into the car. But she did it. She folded the wheelchair and put it in her trunk. Then she drove Victor to the township office.

Thanks to Mrs. Dixon, Victor took the first step to clear up the problem. There was a lot of red tape to deal with. A few days later, Victor had to tell his story in municipal court. The flower woman didn't show up to tell her side.

"You have a right to do business on that corner," the judge explained to Victor. "You have a business license and you pay rent. Don't worry. The court will back you up."

The next morning, Victor got in the van and rode to his corner. When he arrived, a police car was already there. Victor watched as the officers put the flower woman inside the police car. He saw the woman give him a dirty look.

"OK, you're back in business!" the police officer called out to Victor. Then the car pulled away with the woman in the back seat.

Victor had his corner back. But it had taken a week. He had lost a whole week of work. That could be enough to sink anyone's new business. But not Victor's. He decided then and there that he would carry on no matter what.

A few days later, an interesting visitor stopped at Victor's flower stand.

"I see you here every day," said the man. "You seem to do a pretty good business. I was wondering—you don't sell anything besides flowers, do you?"

"No, just roses and mixed bunches," said Victor.

The man shook Victor's hand. "My name is Hal Fanelli," he said. "How do you feel about balloons? I ask because I sell helium gas tanks and toy balloons. I'd like to set you up with a balloon business."

"I hadn't thought about selling anything but flowers," Victor said.

"It's easy," said Mr. Fanelli. "I mean, there's an art to filling a balloon just right. But you could sell those babies like hotcakes right here at your stand. And you could take them to parades and fairs."

"As you can see, sir, I'm in a wheelchair," said Victor. "I couldn't very well haul a big helium tank to a parade."

"I could help you with that, too," said Mr. Fanelli. He pulled out a piece of paper. He showed Victor how much he could make each week by selling different numbers of toy balloons.

Victor began to like the idea very much. "But I would have to get another bank loan," he told the man.

Mr. Fanelli had an answer to the

money problem, too. He said that his company would let Victor pay for the tank little by little.

Victor took care of two customers. Then, right on the spot, he made a deal with Mr. Fanelli.

Later, on the phone, he made a deal with Mr. Houseman, too. Victor could store his helium tank and balloons in the office. They could sit right by the refrigerator. Mr. Houseman would not ask for any extra money. Victor thought that things were looking up. He hoped that having the office might pay off at last.

CHAPTER 9

Fun Times

On Friday morning, Mr. Fanelli came by again. This time he brought along a gas tank on wheels and a box of toy balloons. He set up the tank right beside Victor's chair. Between flower customers, he showed Victor just the right way to fill a balloon with gas.

The balloon had to be held in a certain way. The air had to be let in a certain way. The balloon had to be filled with just exactly the right amount of gas.

Victor tried and tried, but he had trouble getting the hang of it. At one point he said, "I don't think this is going to work out."

"You can do it," said Mr. Fanelli. "Do you know why more people don't sell balloons? Because they didn't bother to learn the right way to do it. You probably think there's only air in a balloon, right? Wrong. Every balloon has *money* in it!"

Victor laughed—and kept trying.

An hour later, Victor clinched the art of filling a balloon with gas. It was a big red balloon with a teddy bear on it. Victor sold that first balloon within 10 minutes.

He filled another balloon, and then another. Mr. Fanelli showed Victor how to tie the balloons together and pull off one at a time. Before long, Victor had a huge bunch of balloons flying 10 feet above the flower stand.

Victor sold a lot of balloons that day. People pulled over when they saw the balloons dancing in the air. Often they wound up buying flowers, too. Victor sold out of balloons *and* flowers.

At the end of the day, Victor pushed and pulled the gas tank into the office. That was the hardest part of the balloon business.

The next weekend was the town's big football parade. Mr. Fanelli picked up Victor and his gas tank early. Then he took them to the parade. He left Victor with a box of balloons shaped like footballs.

Victor got right to work. He filled up one balloon after another. He put together the biggest bunch of balloons the town had ever seen.

Then the crowds came. "Look, Mommy, it's the flower man!" said the first little boy who came by. Victor remembered the child from the flower stand. "Mommy, I want a balloon!" cried the boy.

His mother pulled out her money and gave two dollars to Victor.

"You enjoy that balloon now, you hear?" Victor told the little boy.

Lots of mothers bought balloons for their little boys that day. Fathers bought balloons for their little girls. Parents and grandparents bought balloons for children. Boys bought balloons for their girlfriends. Girls bought balloons for their boyfriends.

Victor made a lot of money at the football parade. When the school band marched down the street, Victor felt as if it was playing just for him. He had never been so happy. The beat of the drums felt just like his heart, beating with joy.

Mr. Fanelli took Victor to other parades. He took Victor to every little town fair. Victor sold balloons on weekends and evenings. He sold balloons at times when it was either too late or too early to sell flowers. And he sold both flowers and balloons at the flower stand. He was having the best time of his life.

One night at home he was adding up his week's earnings when his mother came into the room.

"How is it going, son?" Mrs. Marks asked.

Victor looked up at her. He twirled the pencil in his hand. "Mother, I have some news for you."

"I hope you're going to tell me that you're making as much as you did at the workshop," said Mrs. Marks.

"No," said Victor, pretending to look sad. "I can't tell you that." He watched his mother's face fall. "I'm making *more*. In fact, I'm making twice as much as I did at the workshop!"

Victor's mother grabbed him around the neck and kissed him. "I'm so proud of you!" she said. "I will never again say that you can't do something when you say you can. *Nothing* can hold you back, son!"

"That makes two of us who are proud of you," chimed in Mr. Marks. He had heard them talking. He walked over and shook his son's hand.

"Now I just hope that nothing goes wrong," said Victor. "This flower stand is almost too good to be true!"

"What can go wrong?" Mrs. Marks asked. "Your life is in your own hands for the first time. No one can take that away from you."

"I'm not doing everything on my own," Victor said. "I still need the help of other people, like Mr. Houseman and Mr. Fanelli. And the bank. And you and Dad, of course."

"You've done most of this on your own," said Mr. Marks. "I take my hat off to you, son. And you can count on me to help you whenever I can."

"Same with me," said Mrs. Marks.

Victor smiled. It felt good to know that his parents were behind him.

Two weeks later, Mr. Houseman came to visit the flower stand. It was strange to see him there. The only other time he had been there was to give Victor the key to the office.

"I have some bad news for you," Mr. Houseman began. "A fellow named Morris wants to open a used car lot here. He's willing to pay me full rent. I can't turn him down."

Victor could not believe what he was hearing. He felt as if the bottom had fallen out of his wonderful new world.

C H A P T E R   10

A New Challenge

"So now what happens?" Victor asked Mr. Houseman. "I guess that means I'll have to leave, right?"

"I'm sorry," said Mr. Houseman. "I can't turn down someone who wants to rent the whole lot. I told you up front what the story was."

"That's true," said Victor softly. He was afraid he was going to cry. That was the last thing he wanted to do.

Then Victor remembered his lease. "What about my lease?" he asked. "I do have a lease, you know."

"Your lease runs out the end of next month," said Mr. Houseman. "Sure, you can stay until then. That will give you time to look for a new place."

Victor was discouraged. He had accomplished so much. He had started his own business from scratch. He had stopped someone from trying to steal away his customers. He had even worked out a way to make extra money selling balloons. But having to leave the corner of Route 20 and Wood Street was the biggest problem yet. He could never find another corner that good.

Most of all, Victor was angry with himself. He felt like a fool. How could he have let himself believe that the corner would always be his? All day he kept asking himself that question over and over.

Victor didn't bring balloons to the park

the next morning. He had to take another scouting trip around the area. He needed to find another perfect corner for his flower stand.

Victor spent the morning taking two bus rides, one on each side of Route 20. He saw empty lots, but they were miles away from Wholesale Flowers. He saw no perfect corners.

Along the way, Victor did see a young woman selling flowers. Her stand was not on an empty corner, however. It sat on the edge of a busy used car lot.

If I can't go through it, I'll go around it. Victor heard his own words dancing across his brain. Seeing that flower stand on a used car lot gave him an idea. "Why can't I just stay where I am?" he thought.

Mr. Houseman had said that the car dealer's name was Morris. As soon as Victor got home that night, he called his landlord.

"I don't know if Mr. Morris would want

me to give anyone his phone number," said Mr. Houseman. "But I can give him *your* number. If he wants to talk, he can call you."

Victor waited and waited by the phone. He could hear the television in the living room. Victor waited at the phone through three TV shows. He was beginning to feel down again.

"Mr. Morris isn't going to call," Victor said to himself at last. He turned the chair toward the door. He moved away from the phone and was almost in the next room when the phone rang. Victor buzzed right back. It was Mr. Morris.

"I'll give you 10 percent of my take," Victor began. "I'll sit on the corner selling flowers and balloons. I need just enough space in the office for a refrigerator and a gas tank."

Mr. Morris thought about it. "I'm just getting started in the used car business," he said. "A little help with the rent would be great."

"Then we have a deal?" Victor held his breath.

"Sure. It's a deal," said Mr. Morris. "Maybe your flowers and balloons will draw people in to look at my cars! And please call me Randy. We'll be seeing a lot of each other."

Victor let out his breath. What a relief! He saw that he was jumping up and down in his chair.

Randy Morris began bringing in cars a few weeks later. Victor stayed on with his flowers and balloons.

When the lot was full of used cars, Randy held a grand opening party. He bought 200 balloons from Victor. Randy tied them to a line running along two sides of the lot.

It was a fine party. Mr. Houseman and Mr. Fanelli were there, along with many other people.

"I sold two cars today," Randy said to Victor. "That makes me pretty happy. But look at you. You sold *dozens* of flowers and balloons! You have a very nice little business going here. You were smart to work out a deal so you could stay."

"Well, you know the old saying," said Victor. "If you can't go through a problem, go around it."

"I'll have to remember that," said Randy. "That's a good one."